A Good Day's Work

**Sheila Hollins, Shirley-Anne Wheeler
and Wayne McGregor
illustrated by Rachael Ball**

Series Consultant: Kathy Melling

Beyond Words

London

7

22

First published in the UK 2018 by Books Beyond Words.

Text & illustrations © Books Beyond Words, 2018.

ISBN 978-1-78458-100-8

British Library Cataloguing-in-Publication Data

A catalogue record for this book is available from the British Library.

Printed by Lamport Gilbert Ltd, Reading.

Books Beyond Words is a Community Interest Company registered in England and Wales (7557861).

Further information about the Books Beyond Words series can be obtained from Beyond Words' website: www.booksbeyondwords.co.uk.

Contents

A Good Day's Work

Work is a big part of life for both John and Daisy. They get some very important benefits from work, like friendship and money to spend on the things they want. There are responsibilities too, like being on time, following policies like health and safety, and working well as a team. *A Good Day's Work* shows John and Daisy taking pride in their jobs and understanding their responsibilities well, so that they can sort out problems when they crop up. The stories can be read together or on their own to help someone think about what the day-to-day reality of having a job is like, or to talk about their own situations and responsibilities and how they can make sure they are getting the most from their job.

Reading Books Beyond Words to help think about work

This mini series of four books has been co-created with people with learning disabilities to help young people and adults think about work and to imagine themselves in work. These straightforward picture stories introduce practical information about choosing and getting a job, about settling in and doing a job, and about enjoying being in work.

The stories are based on issues that affect many people who we think will find the books' approach relevant and helpful, including young people with special educational needs and those with a range of impairments and health conditions.

You won't find every possible work situation or choice in these stories. Rather they can help the person or group you are supporting to reflect on their own hopes and experiences, even if they are quite different from what's in the story. This way you can start conversations about what people want to do themselves, or what work is like for them. Many readers like to name the people in the story. This can increase empathy with *all* the characters and help readers to think about even minor characters' stories and choices.

If you are reading this book in a community, school or college book club, you might consider inviting a work advisor to come and meet the group, to hear their ideas and answer any questions they have. This can also be an opportunity for individual members to arrange an appointment with the advisor to explore their own work aspirations further.

Why are there no words?

Many people find pictures much easier for following stories or learning new information than words, whether written or spoken. It's tempting to think that pictures are for children and are just a means to learn to read, but this isn't true. From the earliest times people have used pictures to pass on stories from generation to generation, or to give meaningful instructions where words are confusing; think about the way that pictures and diagrams are used in everyday situations to give instructions for cooking, crafts or building flat-pack furniture. Getting meaning from pictures is an essential skill, and one we learn early on.

Words, on the other hand, can create a barrier for people who find it hard to read, or they can put off people who had a difficult time at school with words and literacy. Combining words and pictures can also make understanding harder for some people, even if they are good readers.

How to read stories told in pictures

The most important thing to remember is that every reader will create a different version of the story. This is fine. There is no right or wrong story; what matters is the one that makes sense to the particular person or group exploring what work means to them. Your story – if you are a support worker, parent or job coach – is your own, and may be quite different from the one the reader sees.

Giving up control over the story can be difficult; staying quiet and letting the person explore the

46

pictures is a skill that takes practice. Gentle prompts will usually give you a lot more information about the reader than supplying fixed answers.

Making it real

Individual readers will have different starting points. For example, some people start with the 'action' in the picture, noticing what people are doing or where they are, and often wanting to give names to all of the characters. This is useful to provide context. Other layers of reading include what characters are thinking, feeling or saying.

An important moment when reading together is to notice when to make the switch from the fiction of the narrative in the story to real-life situations. We can do this with a graded set of questions that move the focus of the conversation from what's happening in the story to what a reader's own ideas, hopes and aspirations might be.

We call this the 'exploratory' or 'predictive' level of reading, where we start to imagine or predict things that are not in the story but can be related to our own lives.

To support the switch from fiction to reality:

1. start with "who?" and "what?" questions: "Who is that?" "What is happening?" "What are they doing?"

2. move on to more open prompts such as "I wonder what it would be like to ... be a volunteer/be at work"

3. switch to making the link with the person's own experiences and thoughts, for example: "Would you like to ... volunteer/work?" "Has that happened to you?"

Extending the reading to practical activities

Here are some ideas for creative ways to build on the story created and to support and develop people's ideas about work.

Together on a big sheet of paper draw an outline of someone with a job/without a job – this could be a photo of the person themselves. Note what feelings and activities the person associates with work, any worries or hopes, or steps they might take to prepare for work.

Draw a 'Me Map' or spider diagram with a photo of the person in the middle and a title like: 'What will help me think about getting a job'/'What will help me think about volunteering'. List all the things that the person wants to learn or try out as part of their journey towards work. Some people might like to use pictures from magazines or the internet.

Take photos of people in a 'freeze frame', like a statue of a person in different situations: before going to work, getting ready in the morning, travelling to work, and at work. You could use pictures from these books as models. Use these freeze frames as key points along a timeline of a day at work, drawn on a long sheet of paper. The timeline could include different people you might meet along the way, what you might talk to them about, things you look forward to during the day, and what your job might be.

Supporting an individual or members of a group to start thinking about work

You can help each person to think about themselves as someone who could have a job and a career, and could make a valuable contribution to the workplace. Here are some group activities which can help to build people's confidence in their own transferable skills and personal qualities. In each case, you can give as much support with reading or writing or choosing a picture as each member needs.

Write each person's name at the top of a piece of paper or card. Pass the paper/card around the group for other people to add a word or picture showing what they like about the person, or something that person is good at. When everyone has added something to the list, each person reads out what is on their own paper/card, with help if needed, finding out how other people see them, and giving them the opportunity to think and talk about themselves in a positive way.

Building on the activity above, ask people to think about their interests, hobbies and other things they are good at. Help them use these ideas to make a collage with pictures of their preferred activities or a spider diagram using words or drawings if they prefer. Share each collage or spider diagram with the group, and think together about what jobs people can do that fit with their skills and interests.

The right to work and mental wellbeing

Everyone has the right to work. Our job and our career are often a big part of who we are and how we think about ourselves. Work also brings with it important benefits like money, social capital and wellbeing. People with learning disabilities have the same rights as everyone else, and the evidence shows that starting work with a supportive employer is the best way to support them to take up their right to work. This gives them the chance to take their place as active members of their communities and wider society, as well as bring a rich variety of skills and talents to the workplace.

It is known that being in work can have a positive effect on our wellbeing. As well as providing money and other things we need for daily life, it can bring self-esteem, companionship and status. Having a job gives:

- opportunities for social contacts and support

- structure to how we use our time

- physical and mental activity

- the chance to develop skills

- a sense of identity and personal achievement

- greatly increased confidence and a feeling of 'being like everyone else'.

These can also be important in helping the recovery of people who are mentally and/or physically unwell.

Supported employment

Finding and getting a job can be scary, especially if you have no experience of being in the workplace. Starting a job can be a confusing experience, and it's common to feel anxious, uncertain and tired. For many people with a learning disability, good employment support is critical to getting and keeping a job.

People with learning disabilities may need good quality welfare benefit advice to understand the financial benefits and implications of working. Most people will get more money in a full-time job than if they do not work. They may also be able to keep some of their benefits if they get a job, such as Disability Living Allowance (DLA) or Personal Independence Payment (PIP). Good advice will include 'better-off calculations' for people to see whether there will be more advantages to being in work rather than living on welfare benefits.

Supported employment, or job coaching, has for many years been a successful way of supporting people with learning disabilities to get and keep paid jobs. The model uses a partnership approach to help people find employment that lasts, and to help businesses employ valuable workers. Supported employment does not focus on getting people 'ready' for work through training or basic qualifications; it is about giving good quality, person-centred support to find the right job for the right person, then getting training and support in place to help them enjoy work and stay there. This is called place, train and maintain. The diagram on page 52 shows how the approach works.

Developing a career

Arranging the right support

Getting the right worker

Getting the right job

Getting to know the job

Agreeing a plan together

Understanding needs

Getting to know the person

Employer

Employee

**The Supported
Employment Model**

Supported employment is based on the following principles:

- everyone can work if they want to, in the right job with the right support

- everyone can make a positive contribution in the workplace

- people need real jobs, where wages are paid at the going rate with the same terms and conditions as other employees.

It is easy to make assumptions about the jobs that people can do, which may not take into account the full range of talent and skill that they have. The first step in good supported employment is to get to know the person and understand their experience, skills, abilities, interests, wishes and needs. This is known as vocational profiling. This process helps to identify the range of jobs that may be a good match for the person, and it may take some creative thinking as to how people's skills and talents can benefit employers and their businesses. Giving people information and experiences in work is helpful as part of getting to know them. This may involve positive risk-taking so that people are supported to use their choice and control to achieve their career aspirations.

Employers are recognised as equal customers in the process, and should be supported to understand the business case for a diverse workforce, including people with learning disabilities. There are clear benefits for employers in working with supported employment:

- a free job-matching service which can help to reduce their recruitment costs and staff turn-over

- motivated employees who will be committed to their business

- an enhanced reputation, both internally and with customers.

Employing a diverse workforce can also lead to innovation in the employer's products and services. It can improve morale and team working, as well as demonstrating a company's corporate social responsibility. Supported employment aims to develop long-term relationships with employers so that companies approach them for staff prior to going to advert. This helps to maximise the company's savings.

The social model of disability and Equality Law both highlight the need to remove barriers to participation. Bringing about equality in employment for people with learning disabilities may mean changing the way work is structured, taking away physical barriers and/or providing extra support for a job applicant or worker. It is the role of supported employment to help employers see the benefits of adapting their recruitment and selection processes, and using methods such as working interviews or work trials. Working interviews are an alternative to formal interviews, and give the person an opportunity to demonstrate their skills in the workplace. The employer can observe and evaluate using much the same criteria as they use to judge interview performance. A work trial is a way of trying out a potential employee before offering them a job. Both of these methods are viewed as a reasonable adjustment to the recruitment and selection process.

The aim of job matching is to ensure that employers get the right worker and people with learning disabilities get the right job. This may involve either carving or customising jobs. Jobs can be 'carved' by selecting and combining duties from one or more existing jobs into a new position. Jobs can be customised based on an individualised match between the strengths and interests of a job seeker and the identified business needs of an employer.

When someone has been successful in getting a job, both they and their employer will be given support to make sure the new worker learns their job to the employer's standards and integrates socially into their workplace. This may involve adapting standard training and induction processes, or providing one-to-one support in the workplace. Some specific training for the employer before the person starts will help increase their confidence and understanding of how to work with their new employee.

It is also important to recognise that few people stay in the same job for the whole of their working lives. Everyone must adapt to changing labour markets and many people will want to improve their working lives, and this is no different for people with learning disabilities. Supported employment should encourage career development by making sure that people have good training opportunities and the chance to increase their responsibility at work. This requires long-term support.

Supported employment has a range of benefits. It ensures that people are supported to be full and active members of their workforces and wider communities, both socially and economically. Employment is a valued social role and becoming employed can help change negative perceptions, with wider positive consequences for the person.

Finding the right employment support

Finding good quality support can be difficult. If you aren't eligible for local authority support, this may affect your access to supported employment, and the people with the right expertise might be found in different places, depending on the area you live in. This can include schools, colleges, supported employment agencies, training providers and Jobcentre Plus.

If you need help finding a supported employment provider in your local area, or are finding it hard to get access to the level of support you need to get or stay in work, there are organisations that can help. The British Association of Supported Employment is the national trade association for the sector and maintains a list of local providers, as well as best practice standards and resources (see page 62).

It is important that support is provided by someone who is trained to the National Occupational Standards for Supported Employment Practitioners. Here are some questions you can ask to see if the support on offer from providers is good quality and evidence-based:

- How long have you been supporting people to find and keep jobs?

- Do you believe that everyone who wants to work, can work, with the right job and the right support?

- What types of jobs have you helped people to find? How many hours do they work and what is their rate of pay?

- How will you get to know me?

- How do you let employers know about what you do?

- How will you involve me in the process of finding a job?

- How will you present my skills and abilities to an employer?

- How will you support me to learn my job?

- What support will you give to the employer?

- How will you support me to keep my job and progress my career?

- Will you help me with my benefits to make sure that I am financially better off in work?

- Have you ever supported someone who has a disability similar to mine?

- Have you ever excluded people from using your services? Why?

- Do you have any recommendations from those who use your services, families or employers?

The role of the manager

When an employee with learning disabilities begins their job, they may have additional support from a job coach to settle in and learn the work as part of the staff team. The job coach will also support the employer at the outset to develop their confidence working with the new employee, and to make their processes accessible. This additional support should gradually withdraw, meaning that the new worker's role is established and sustainable. As with any other employee, it is the manager's and employer's responsibility to ensure that they have the structures they need to do their job well in the long term, with the right support, supervision, appraisal and development opportunities.

While this means that an employee with learning disabilities has the same rights and opportunities as their peers, in practice there is no one-size-fits-all approach. Specific adjustments and support structures may be needed for each employee, and it's important not to make assumptions about what will help, but to get to know each person individually.

Good and consistent communication will be key to supporting an employee. Sometimes this will mean information in step-by-step pictorial form or straightforward language. This should apply to supervision and appraisal paperwork, so that the employee has a good idea of what is expected, what is going well and what they need to do differently. It's important not to assume that an employee will automatically know if an aspect of their job is going well or not. Disciplinary and grievance procedures should be accessible too.

Depending on the person, they may need reminding about parts of their job for some time; checking a task list may be a long-term feature of their role. If something goes wrong, or they do a part of the job badly, it may be important to talk to the employee about it in private as soon as possible, rather than pretending it hasn't happened or dealing with it at a later time. This talk should also be an opportunity to find a solution or a new way of doing something that the employee can understand and stick to.

In any job things are likely to change for a number of reasons, including staff turnover, change of premises or new business methods. These sorts of changes may be challenging for all staff; they should be encouraged to offer natural support to each other, and everyone should have access to the same training and support to deal with new aspects of their work. Employees with learning disabilities and/or autism may need additional support or supervision to manage changes in their job, or a longer time to learn and adjust to doing things differently.

Nevertheless it's important not to assume that an employee will want to keep doing the same job for the duration of their employment. It is the role of their manager to recognise good quality work and achievement, and encourage aspiration. They should offer training and development, including accreditation and promotion where relevant, and make sure that employees with learning disabilities have as much opportunity as they need to build a successful and rewarding career.

Having a job: an interview with Emily Bilham

An extract from a talk by Emily about her own experiences of work, given to students at Fairfield Farm College, Wiltshire.

How did you feel when you first started your job? How do you feel now?

When I first started my job I felt quite anxious and uncertain about what was expected of me, but my boss is very supportive and made sure I understood what was required of me. I also got quite tired.

However now I am familiar with my roles and responsibilities and I know the building and all the people who work in the building so I actually look forward to work and feel confident in what I have to do. I don't feel anxious any more.

What is the hardest thing about having a job? How do you deal with it?

The hardest thing is the responsibility and having to be organised. As part of my job I do health and safety checks at a medical centre. I recognise that the things I check are really important and that I have to check them properly to make sure that everyone stays safe.

It's hard to be organised all the time. You need to make sure that you get there on time. You need to plan your holidays and the rest of your life around work because that comes first.

What would you say are the three most important skills needed to be successful in a workplace?

- Being reliable – an employer wants to know that they can rely on you to do your job at the right time, in the right place and to do the things that are needed.

- Being organised.

- Enjoying your job – if you enjoy your job and take pride in what you do everyone will see that and you will do a good job.

What advice would you give to someone who is about to enter the world of work for the first time?

- Having a job and being part of the workforce is great. It makes you feel good about yourself and that you are doing something useful.

- Apply for jobs that you are interested in and have the skills to do well.

- You learn new things when you are working.

- Always be interested and enthusiastic about what you do.

- And of course it's always good to get a salary into your bank account!

Useful resources in the UK

British Association for Supported Employment (BASE)
www.base-uk.org
A membership organisation that exists to develop and encourage best practice in supported employment, through advising on policy development and providing information, training and consultancy. A list of their current member organisations who provide supported employment services can be found on their website. Each of these organisations is working in some way to support people with disabilities or other disadvantages into sustainable employment.
Tel: 01204 880733
admin@base-uk.org

Mencap
www.mencap.org.uk
A national organisation aiming to improve the lives of people with learning disabilities and autism and their families. Mencap conducts research and campaigns and offers advice, resources and support, including a national Helpline. Via its network of local member organisations, Mencap provides direct services to people and their families, including social activities, learning and employment support.
Helpline: 0808 808 1111
helpline@mencap.org.uk

Jobcentre Plus
www.gov.uk/contact-jobcentre-plus
If you are over 18, your local Jobcentre can help you learn new skills and find a job, tell you about

disability-friendly employers in your area and discuss other support that may be available to you. You may wish to make an appointment to see a disability employment advisor, who will be able to give you personalised advice. You find contact details for your nearest Jobcentre branch online.

Citizens Advice Bureau
www.citizensadvice.org.uk
Citizens Advice provides free, confidential and independent advice online, over the phone and in person in their local branches. Advisors can inform you about your rights and talk to you about any problems you are facing in the workplace and how to solve them. You can search online to find contact details for your nearest branch.
Tel (England): 03444 111 444
Tel (Wales): 03444 77 20 20

The National Autistic Society (NAS)
www.autism.org.uk
A national charity providing information, support and specialist services as well as campaigning to improve the lives of people with autism (including Asperger syndrome) and their families. NAS has a network of support centres and enterprise activities that give people the opportunity to develop their skills, prepare for work and find a job they can do well and enjoy. NAS also offers information, advice and training for employers to guide them in how to recruit and best support autistic employees.
Helpline: 0808 800 4104
nas@nas.org.uk

Scope

www.scope.org.uk

A national disability charity who provide information about work and employment for people with disabilities on their website. The charity also offers online employment support via their Support to Work scheme.

www.scope.org.uk/support/disabled-people/work

Tel: 0300 222 5742

supporttowork@scope.org.uk

ENABLE Scotland

www.enable.org.uk

A Scottish charity working to improve the lives of people with a learning disability and their families. Through the ENABLE Works service, adults and young people can access support to prepare for the workplace and find the job that's right for them. Employers can also get advice and support to help them recruit and retain staff with learning disabilities.

Tel: 0300 0200 101

enabledirect@enable.org.uk

Disability Law Service

www.dls.org.uk

A charity providing free legal information, advice and representation to people with disabilities and their families. If you feel that you have been discriminated against because of your disability you can contact the DLS for advice.

Tel: 0207 791 9800

advice@dls.org.uk

People First
www.peoplefirstinfo.org.uk
A national self-advocacy organisation offering lots of useful information about many aspects of work and employment for people with disabilities, including employment rights, finding work, starting and running your own business and volunteering.
www.peoplefirstinfo.org.uk/work-and-learning/accessing-work.aspx

National Development Team for inclusion (NDTi)
www.ndti.org.uk
NDTi is a not-for-profit organisation that exists to ensure that people with disabilities and older people have choice and control over their own lives. They carry out policy development, consultancy, training, research and evaluation around different issues including employment.
Tel: 01225 789135
office@ndti.org.uk

Learning Disability England
www.learningdisabilityengland.org.uk
A membership organisation working to make the voices of people with learning disabilities heard through campaigning, consultancy and training. They can also offer advice to their members on issues including person-centred support and engaging people with learning disabilities in communities.
Tel: 0300 201 0455
info@LDEngland.org.uk

Related titles in the Books Beyond Words series

Rose Gets in Shape (2016) by Roger Banks and Paul Wallang, illustrated by Mike Nicholson. Rose lives on her own and she has picked up some bad habits about eating and taking exercise. Her energy is low and she gets tired easily. When her doctor tells her that her weight is causing health problems she decides to get in shape. We follow Rose through the struggles and triumphs of her weight loss journey, the new activities she takes up, and the good friends and support she finds along the way.

George Gets Smart (2001) by Sheila Hollins, Margaret Flynn and Philippa Russell, illustrated by Catherine Brighton. George's life changes when he learns how to keep clean and smart. People no longer avoid being with him and he enjoys the company of his workmates and friends.

Belonging (2018) Sheila Hollins, Valerie Sinason and Access All Areas artists, illustrated by Lucy Bergonzi. Kali is lonely. She has no real friends and no reason to leave the house to socialise; community activities seem remote and pointless to her. Outside her home, Kali defends herself with a mask of hostility, hiding her true feelings. But when things go wrong, Kali finds herself in a position to help Stefan, another vulnerable and lonely person. In the aftermath, they forge a friendship and begin to find themselves in the centre of a community where they feel they belong.

Speaking Up for Myself (reissued 2017) by Sheila Hollins, Jackie Downer, Linnett Farquarson and Oyepeju Raji, illustrated by Lisa Kopper. Having a learning disability and being from an ethnic minority group can make it hard to get good services. Natalie learns to fix problems by being assertive and getting help from someone she trusts.

Michelle Finds a Voice (2016, 2nd edition) by Sheila Hollins and Sarah Barnett, illustrated by Denise Redmond. Michelle cannot speak and is unable to communicate her thoughts and feelings. She feels isolated and unhappy. Michelle and her carers try signing, symbols and electronic aids to find a solution that works.

Authors and artist

Sheila Hollins is Emeritus Professor of Psychiatry of Disability at St George's, University of London, after a distinguished career as a Consultant Psychiatrist in the NHS. She is a past President of the Royal College of Psychiatrists and of the BMA. She is the founder, editor and Executive Chair for Books Beyond Words, a family carer and sits in the House of Lords.

Shirley-Anne Wheeler manages the Equals Employment Service as part of the Integrated Learning Disabilities Team in Enfield, North London. She has worked as an Occupational Therapist in various settings for over 25 years, primarily raising the aspirations of people with learning disabilities and promoting their independence.

Wayne McGregor is a counter assistant and a dancer with a positive and flexible approach to life. He has worked for Sainsbury's for five years, where he enjoys serving customers. He is also a long-standing member of the Baked Bean Dance Company where he has performed alongside Hugh Grant.

Rachael Ball is a cartoonist and teacher. Her first graphic novel, *The Inflatable Woman*, was published in 2015 by Bloomsbury and listed as a Guardian Best Graphic Novel of 2015. Her second graphic novel *Wolf* is due for release in September 2018 (Self Made Hero). Her work has also appeared in cult 90's comic *Deadline*, and she has illustrated for various publications. Rachael also coordinates the London branch of Laydeez do Comics, which promotes women in comics.

Kathy Melling has worked in the supported employment sector since the late 1970s, first in the US, studying under Marc Gold, the founder of Training in Systematic Instruction and supported employment at the University of Illinois. She emigrated to the UK in the early 1980s and her pioneering work in Kent, transforming day services and developing supported employment, featured in the King's Fund 'Changing Days' research project. She became the National Employment Lead for Valuing People Now in 2009, and helped establish the British Association of Supported Employment, where she is still an active member of the National Executive Committee. She now works as an independent trainer and consultant, working on the introduction of National Occupational Standards and leading on employment and supported internships for the Preparing for Adulthood programme.

Acknowledgments

We are grateful to Emily Bilham for additional text in this book, and for the advice and support of our advisory group: Shlomo Weltman, Daniel Yefet, Emily Bilham, Tim Bilham, Barry Stanley-Wilkinson, Milly Wheeler, Clive Heslop, Francesca Capelli, Antoinette Cole, Quilenn Huntesmith, Fiona Taylor.

Many thanks to all individuals and groups who trialled the pictures, including Bromley Speaking Up Group, Advocacy for All: Anne Berry, Edward Hamilton, Jonathan Brinson, Holly Pace, Teresa Durman; Hannah O'Dwyer, Bernie O'Dwyer; Bromley Mencap Step Forward Programme: Mark Cayzar, Polly Sharpey, Marilyn Searle, Luke Chandler, Lee Champion; Whitehorse Hub at Croydon Central Library: Tina, Ian, David, Jacqui, Lloyd, Sarah; Northamptonshire Adult Social Services Olympus LIVE: Jane Cryer, Holly Burgess, Anthony Pond; The Square Peg Company: Autumn Fawcett, Joanne Clair, Josh Elliott, Emily Curry, Claire Kirchoff; Stonewater: Scott Grimley; Stonewater, Bow Court: Tammy Peapell; Hamilton Lodge School and College, Brighton; Islington Council; Keyring Supported Living: Debbie Catlin, Jeanie Smith; Pepenbury; Jill Singh; Pluss, Plymouth People First: Darren, Scott, Adam, Mark, Abigail, Bob, John, Amy, Jason; The Vine, Plymouth People First: Elaine, Deborah, Albina, Alison, Queensmill School: Jupiter, Mars, Neptune and Q6 Classes.

Finally we are grateful to the Department for Work and Pensions for their generous financial support of this book and wider project.

Beyond Words: publications and training

Books Beyond Words are stories for anyone who finds pictures easier than words. A list of all Beyond Words publications, including print and eBook versions of Books Beyond Words titles, and where to buy them, can be found on our website:

www.booksbeyondwords.co.uk

Workshops for family carers, support workers and professionals about using Books Beyond Words are provided regularly in London, or can be arranged on request in other localities or to cover specific areas of interest. Self-advocates are welcome. For information about forthcoming training please contact us:

email: admin@booksbeyondwords.co.uk

Video clips showing our books being read are also on our website and YouTube channel: www.youtube.com/user/booksbeyondwords and on our DVD, *How to Use Books Beyond Words*.

How to read this book

This is a story for people who find pictures easier to understand than words. It is not necessary to be able to read any words at all.

1. Some people are not used to reading books. Start at the beginning and read the story in each picture. Encourage the reader to hold the book themselves and to turn the pages at their own pace.

2. Whether you are reading the book with one person or with a group, encourage them to tell the story in their own words. You will discover what each person thinks is happening, what they already know, and how they feel. You may think something different is happening in the pictures yourself, but that doesn't matter. Wait to see if their ideas change as the story develops. Don't challenge the reader(s) or suggest their ideas are wrong.

3. Some pictures may be more difficult to understand. It can help to prompt the people you are supporting, for example:

- I wonder who that is?
- I wonder what is happening?
- What is he or she doing now?
- I wonder how he or she is feeling?
- Do you feel like that? Has it happened to you/ your friend/ your family?

4. You don't have to read the whole book in one sitting. Allow people enough time to follow the pictures at their own pace.

5. Some people will not be able to follow the story, but they may be able to understand some of the pictures. Stay a little longer with the pictures that interest them.